BREAD & BAKING

PARRAGON

Contents

Introduction

At one time considered an outdated pursuit, making bread and baking cakes has gained in popularity and become a pleasure enjoyed by millions. The increased awareness of the benefits of home-baking is in many ways due to the large supermarkets offering a product which may have a good shelf life, but often has little in the way of taste or character. Although many supermarkets are now attempting to rectify this situation, the prices charged for the better quality products makes home-baking a far more attractive option.

Many people who have never attempted to bake their own bread consider it something of an art, although in reality baking bread simply requires a little skill and the implementation of a few rules. When making yeasted doughs, remember that yeast is a living organism and to work it needs warmth, food and moisture. This is provided by blending it with warm water or milk and sugar. It is important that the liquid is not too hot or the yeast will be killed and the dough will not rise at all. The dough should be left, covered, for a hour or two in a warm place, until it has doubled in size. If the dough is left for too long, it will over work and the finished loaf will not be very risen and will have a slightly sour taste. It is then kneaded thoroughly, called 'knocking back' or 'punching down', to distribute the yeast and improve the elasticity of the dough. The dough is then shaped and left to rise for a second time, until almost doubled in size again – this takes about half the time of the first rising. Baking is carried out at a high temperature to kill the yeast and stop the dough from rising further. In the first stage of cooking, the dough rises rapidly before it sets and finally becomes crusty. To test if bread is cooked, tap the base with the knuckles and if it sounds hollow it is ready.

Bread and Baking contains over fifty delicious recipes, including Indian fried breads such as Loochis and Batura, popular flat breads like Chapatties and Naan, and yeastless breads such as Corn Bread and Soda Bread. Sweet recipes are covered, too, with recipes for favourites like muffins and teabreads, as well as other tea-time treats such as Crumpets, Victoria Sandwich, Treacle Tart and Apple Strudel. All the recipes are set out in an easy-to-follow format and have been kitchen-tested to give perfect results every time.

There is nothing more wholesome and appetising than the smell of freshly-baked bread, and nothing more enticing than indulging in fresh home-made scones, buns and cakes. So give yourself the best, and discover the delights of *Bread and Baking*; with recipes from America, France, Italy, Poland, India and Germany as well as Great Britain, you'll be spoilt for choice.

Quick Home-Made Bread

The molasses in this recipe gives the bread an attractive appearance.

MAKES 3 LOAVES

1 tbsp molasses
1 tbsp sunflower oil
1150ml/2 pints lukewarm water
1.5kg/3¼lbs 100% wholemeal flour
2 sachets fast action yeast
3 tsps sea salt

1. Oil 3 × 900g/2lb bread tins and set aside to warm.

2. Add the molasses and oil to half the water, mix and set aside.

3. Place the flour, yeast and salt into a large bowl and mix together thoroughly.

4. Gradually pour the water and molasses mixture into the flour, mixing in with your hands.

5. Add the remaining water bit by bit until the dough is wettish, but not sticky. You may have some water left over.

6. Knead the dough about a dozen times, divide between the three tins and press down firmly. Cover with a damp cloth.

7. Leave to rise in a warm place for 5-10 minutes or until the dough has risen near to the top of the tins.

8. Bake in an oven preheated to 220°C/425°F/Gas Mark 7, for 35-40 minutes or until the loaves sound hollow when tapped underneath.

TIME: Preparation takes 20 minutes, cooking takes 35-40 minutes.

TO FREEZE: This bread will freeze well. Seal in freezer bags.

SULTANA SODA BREAD

Soda bread is a traditional Irish bread which contains no yeast, the bicarbonate of soda and the sour milk are the raising agents here.

MAKES 1 LOAF

460g/1lb plain white flour
1 tsp salt
1 tsp bicarbonate of soda
1 tsp cream of tartar
1 level tbsp sugar
90g/3oz sultanas
280ml/½ pint sour milk or fresh milk mixed with 1 tbsp yogurt

1. Sift the flour, salt, bicarbonate of soda and cream of tartar into a mixing bowl. Stir in sugar and sultanas then add the milk, mixing to form a firm, but not too stiff dough.

2. Knead lightly on a floured board and form into a slightly flattened round. Cut a deep cross on the top and brush the surface with milk.

3. Place on a greased and lightly floured baking sheet and bake in centre of a preheated oven at 200°C/400°F/Gas Mark 6, for 25 minutes.

4. Turn the loaf upside down on the tray and return to oven for a further 5 minutes. The loaf is done if it sounds hollow when tapped on the base.

5. Wrap in a damp cloth and place on its side to cool.

TIME: Preparation takes 15 minutes and cooking takes 30 minutes.

VARIATION: Use other dried fruit in place of the sultanas.

Granary Rolls

For a crisp crust, brush the rolls with salted water and sprinkle with cracked wheat before baking.

SERVES 10

340g/12oz granary flour
1 tsp salt
30g/1oz butter or margarine
15g/½oz fresh yeast or 2 tsps dried yeast
1 tsp brown sugar
225ml/8 fl oz lukewarm water

1. Place the granary flour and salt in a mixing bowl and leave in a warm place.

2. Melt the butter in a pan and leave to cool.

3. Cream the yeast and sugar together with three-quarters of the warm water. Leave in a warm place until bubbly.

4. Make a well in the middle of the flour and pour in the yeast mixture.

5. Add the melted fat and mix to a pliable dough, adding the remaining water as necessary.

6. Knead lightly for 1-2 minutes.

7. Cover with a clean tea-towel and leave in a warm place until the dough has doubled in size.

8. Knead again for 3-5 minutes and shape into 10 smooth rolls.

9. Place well apart on a floured baking tray, cover and leave in a warm place until the rolls have doubled in size.

10. Bake in the centre of a preheated oven, at 220°C/425°F/Gas Mark 7 for 15-20 minutes or until the rolls sound hollow when tapped underneath.

11. Cool on a wire rack.

TIME: Preparation and proving takes about 2 hours, cooking takes 15-20 minutes.

TO FREEZE: The rolls will freeze well for up to 1 month. Allow to thaw for 1 hour at room temperature before use.

Chocolate Cinnamon Sweet Bread

Pull this bread apart to serve in individual pieces rather than slicing it. For a savoury version substitute Parmesan and herbs for the sugar and spice.

MAKES 1 LOAF

Dough
100g/3½oz sugar
1 envelope dry yeast
60ml/4 tbsps warm water
340-400g/12-14oz strong flour
Pinch salt
75g/2½oz butter, softened
5 eggs

Topping
225g/8oz sugar
2 tsps cinnamon
2 tsps cocoa
45g/6 tbsps finely chopped nuts
120g/4oz butter, melted

1. Sprinkle 1 tbsp of the sugar and all the yeast on top of the water and leave it in a warm place until foaming.

2. Sift 340g/12oz of the flour into a bowl and add the remaining sugar and salt. Rub in the butter until completely blended.

3. Add 2 of the eggs and the yeast mixture, mixing in well. Add the remaining eggs one at a time until the mixture forms a soft, spongy dough. Add the remaining flour as necessary. Knead for 10 minutes on a lightly floured surface until smooth and elastic.

4. Place the dough in a greased bowl and turn over to grease all the surfaces. Cover loosely and leave to stand in a warm place for 1-1½ hours, or until doubled in bulk.

5. Butter a ring mould liberally. Knock the dough down and knead it again for about 5 minutes. Shape into balls about 5cm/2-inches in diameter. Mix the topping ingredients together except for the melted butter. Roll the dough balls in the butter and then in the sugar mixture.

6. Layer up the dough balls in the bottom of the mould. Cover and allow to rise again for about 15 minutes. Bake in a preheated 180°C/350°F/Gas Mark 4 oven for about 45-50 minutes. Loosen from the tin and turn out while still warm.

TIME: Preparation takes about 2 hours and cooking takes about 45-50 minutes.

COOK'S TIP: Check the temperature of the water carefully. If it is too hot it will kill the yeast and the bread will not rise.

SERVING IDEAS: Serve warm with coffee or tea, or serve as an accompaniment to a fresh fruit salad.

Wholewheat Brown Bread

This is a very moist bread which will last for days.

MAKES 2 LOAVES

680g/1½lbs wholewheat flour
120g/4oz white flour
100g/3½oz porridge oats
90g/3oz bran
175g/6oz pinhead oatmeal
60g/2oz wheatgerm
½ tsp baking powder
½ tsp salt
1.2 litres/2 pints milk
2 eggs, beaten

1. Mix all the dry ingredients together.

2. Mix the eggs and milk and add to the dry ingredients.

3. Spoon into two greased 460g/1lb loaf tins and bake in the centre of an oven preheated to 180°C/350°F/Gas Mark 4, for 1¼-1½ hours.

4. Turn out to cool on a wire rack.

TIME: Preparation takes about 20 minutes, cooking takes 1¼-1½ hours.

VARIATION: Some caraway seeds can be added to the mixture and some sprinkled on the top before baking.

Scofa Bread

The ideal chunky bread to serve warm with a ploughman's lunch or salads.

MAKES 1 LOAF

570g/1¼lbs self-raising wholemeal flour
225g/8oz bran
1 tsp salt
120g/4oz butter or margarine
Just under 570ml/1 pint water
1 tbsp oil

1. Put the flour, bran and salt into a mixing bowl.

2. Rub in the butter and mix the water and oil together.

3. Make a well in the centre of the flour and pour in the water and oil.

4. Mix in the flour, gradually drawing it into the liquid mixture from the sides, until a dough is formed.

5. Shape into an 18cm/7-inch round and place on a greased baking tray.

6. With a sharp knife mark into four sections, cutting to within 1.2cm/½-inch of the bottom.

7. Bake just above the centre of an oven, preheated to 200°C/400°F/Gas Mark 6, for about 1 hour or until nicely browned and 'hollow' sounding when tapped with the back of your fingers.

8. Remove from the oven and wrap in a clean tea towel to cool.

TIME: Preparation takes 10 minutes, cooking takes 1 hour.

COOK'S TIP: This bread is best eaten within a couple of days.

Soft Bread Rolls

These bread rolls may be split and toasted, buttered and then filled with sizzling cheese or fried eggs to make a nutritious and satisfying snack meal.

MAKES 6

340g/12oz wholewheat flour
1 tsp salt
30g/1oz fresh yeast
1 tsp brown sugar
1 tea cup of milk
30g/1oz butter or margarine.
1 egg, beaten

1. Put the flour and salt in a mixing bowl.

2. Cream the yeast and sugar together until liquid.

3. Warm the milk with the butter.

4. Mix the milk and butter with the creamed yeast and stir in the beaten egg.

5. Make a hollow in the flour and work the milk mixture in gradually to make a soft dough.

6. Knead a little and form into six round cakes.

7. Cover and leave to rise for 20 minutes in a warm place.

8. Bake in an oven preheated to 220°C/425°F/Gas Mark 7 for about 15 minutes.

9. Glaze with beaten egg or milk and sugar a few minutes before removing from the oven.

TIME: Preparation takes 30 minutes, cooking takes 15 minutes.

VARIATION: Make Currant Tea Cakes by adding 90g/3oz currants and 60g/2oz sugar to the recipe in the mixing.

Boston Brown Bread

This traditional American bread is served in Boston with baked beans. However it is equally good served spread with butter for a sweet teabread.

MAKES 1 × 900g/2lb LOAF

15g/½oz butter or margarine
90g/3oz treacle
280ml/½ pint natural yogurt
75g/2½oz wholemeal flour
75g/2½oz plain flour, sieved
90g/3oz cornmeal
1 tsp baking powder
1 tsp salt
60g/2oz raisins

1. Melt the butter in a small pan, add the treacle and heat until softened. Remove from the heat and stir in the yogurt.

2. Put the flours, cornmeal, baking powder and salt into a large mixing bowl. Stir in the raisins, and beat in the yogurt mixture until well combined.

3. Spoon into a lightly greased 900g/2lb loaf tin and level the top. Bake in an oven preheated to 190°C/375°F/Gas Mark 5, for 30 minutes, or until risen and springy to the touch.

4. Cool in the tin for 5 minutes, before turning out onto a wire rack to cool completely.

TIME: Preparation takes about 15 minutes, cooking time is about 30 minutes.

VARIATION: Use other dried fruit instead of raisins.

Corn Bread

This bread is very popular in the Southern States of America.

SERVES 6-8

150g/5oz yellow cornmeal
120g/4oz flour
60g/2oz sugar
1 tsp salt
4 tsps baking powder
1 egg, beaten
225ml/8 fl oz milk
30g/1oz butter, melted

1. Mix the cornmeal, flour, sugar, salt and baking powder in a large bowl.

2. Make a well in the centre and add the egg, milk and melted butter.

3. Beat very well until the ingredients are thoroughly blended.

4. Pour the batter into a greased square baking tin and bake in an oven preheated to 200°C/400°F/Gas Mark 6, for 25-30 minutes, or until risen and golden brown on top.

5. Cut into squares to serve.

TIME: Preparation takes about 15 minutes and cooking takes 25-30 minutes.

VARIATION: Add 30g/1oz grated cheese to the mixture.

Irish Soda Bread

Soda bread is very easy and quick, there is no yeast so the bread does not have to be left to rise.

MAKES 1 LOAF

1 tsp salt
1 tsp sugar
1 heaped tsp cream of tartar
1 heaped tsp bicarbonate of soda
225g/8oz plain white flour
460g/1lb wholemeal flour
460ml/16 fl oz milk mixed with 1 tbsp yogurt

1. Add the salt, sugar, cream of tartar and bicarbonate of soda to the plain white flour and sift into a large mixing bowl. Add wholemeal flour and mix thoroughly with a palette knife, using a lifting motion to aerate the mixture.

2. Make a well in the centre and add milk, mixing until the dough leaves the sides of the bowl clean.

3. Knead into a ball, flatten slightly and place on a greased baking tray. Cut a deep cross into the top of the loaf and brush the top with a little milk. Bake in a preheated oven at 200°C/400°F/Gas Mark 6, for 40 minutes.

4. Remove from the oven, turn loaf upside down and return to the oven for a further five minutes. The loaf is done when it sounds hollow when tapped on the base.

5. Wrap it in a slightly dampened cloth and stand on its side to cool.

TIME: Preparation takes 15 minutes and cooking takes about 45 minutes.

SERVING IDEAS: Cut into quarters, slice and butter generously. Serve with prawns, smoked salmon or fish pâtés, or at tea time with jam.

BREAD

Naan

Naan is traditionally cooked in the Tandoor. It is not difficult to cook naan in a very hot oven, although the distinctive taste of clay cooking will be missing.

MAKES 8 NAAN

460g/1lb plain flour
1 tsp salt
1 tsp kalonji (onion) seeds
1 tsp sugar
1½ sachets fast action or easy blend yeast
90ml/3 fl oz milk
150g/5oz natural yogurt
1 medium-sized egg, beaten
60g/2oz ghee or butter, melted
2 tbsps sesame seeds or white poppy seeds

1. Put the flour, salt, kalonji, sugar and yeast into a large bowl and mix well.

2. Warm the milk until it is lukewarm, reserve 1 tbsp yogurt and add the rest to the milk and blend thoroughly.

3. Add the milk and yogurt mixture, egg and ghee or butter to the flour, knead with your hands, or in a food processor or mixer, until a soft and springy dough is formed.

4. Seal the dough in a large plastic food bag leaving enough room for expansion.

5. Rinse a metal bowl (preferably steel, as this will retain heat better) with hot water and put the bag of dough in it. Put the bowl in a warm place, for ½-1 hour until the dough has risen to double the original quantity.

6. Divide the dough into 8 balls, cover them and keep aside for 10-15 minutes.

7. Preheat an oven to 230°C/450°F/Gas Mark 8 and put an ungreased baking sheet into the oven to preheat for about 10 minutes. Remove the baking sheet from the oven and line with greased greaseproof paper or baking parchment.

8. Take one of the balls and stretch it gently with both hands to make a teardrop shape. Lay this on the baking sheet and press it gently to stretch it to about 15-18cm/6-7 inches in length, maintaining the teardrop shape. Make 2-3 similar shapes at a time and brush with the reserved yogurt, then sprinkle with the sesame or poppy seeds. Bake at the top of the oven for 10-12 minutes, or until puffed and browned.

TIME: Preparation takes 10-15 minutes plus the time needed to prove the dough, cooking takes 20-25 minutes.

SERVING IDEAS: Serve with any meat, chicken or vegetable curry. Suitable for freezing.

VARIATION: Use 1 tsp caraway or cumin seeds instead of the onion seeds while making the dough.

Batura

Batura is a leavened bread which is made from plain flour and then deep-fried. The dough is made with natural yogurt and has a soft, velvet-like texture.

SERVES 6

340g/12oz plain flour
1 tsp salt
2 tsps fast action or easy blend yeast
1 egg, beaten
150g/5oz natural yogurt
2-3 tbsps warm water
Oil for deep frying

1. Put the flour, salt and yeast into a bowl and mix well.

2. Add the egg, yogurt and water and knead until a soft, pliable dough is formed. Alternatively, put all the ingredients into the bowl of a food processor which has a dough hook, and work until the dough is formed.

3. Seal the dough in a large oiled plastic food bag, leaving room for the dough to expand.

4. Put the bag in a steel, metal or cast-iron bowl/saucepan which has been rinsed out with hot water. Leave the dough in a warm place for 35-40 minutes to rise.

5. Remove the dough from the bag and divide it into 6 equal portions.

6. Roll each portion gently between your palms in a circular motion and flatten it into a round cake.

7. Dust the cake lightly in a little flour and roll it out gently to a large circle, about 15cm/6-inch in diameter.

8. Heat the oil to 180°C/350°F; take care not to overheat the oil. Place a batura in the hot oil and fry it for 1 minute; turn it over and fry the other side for a further minute or until it is a rich creamy colour. Drain on kitchen paper.

9. Make and fry all the baturas the same way. It is easier to roll out and fry one batura at a time rather than rolling them all out first.

TIME: Preparation takes 5-10 minutes plus 35-40 minutes for proving the dough, cooking takes 12-15 minutes.

SERVING IDEA: Serve with Indian dishes.

VARIATION: Use equal quantity of plain and wholemeal flour.

Chapatties

A Chapattie is a dry roasted unleavened bread best eaten as soon as it is cooked. They are not very filling, so 2-3 chapatties per person is quite normal.

MAKES 14 CHAPATTIES

340g/12oz fine wholemeal flour or atta/ chapatti flour
½ tsp salt
15g/½oz butter, or ghee
175-280ml/6-10 fl oz warm water (quantity depends on the texture of the flour)
1 tbsp extra flour in a shallow bowl or plate

1. Food Mixer Method: Place the flour, salt and fat together in the bowl and mix thoroughly on a medium-to-low speed taking care to see that all the fat has been well incorporated into the flour. Turn the speed down to minimum and gradually add the water. When a dough is formed, knead it until it is soft and pliable. Cover the dough with a well-moistened cloth and keep aside for ½-1 hour.

2. Hand Method: Put the flour and salt in a large bowl and rub in the fat. Gradually add the water and keep mixing and kneading until a soft and pliable dough is formed. Cover the dough as above and keep aside.

3. Divide the dough into 14 walnut-sized portions. Roll each portion in a circular motion between the palms to make a smooth round ball, then flatten the ball to make a round cake. Dip each cake into the dry flour and roll the chapatti into a disc of about 15cm/6-inch diameter.

4. An iron griddle is normally used for cooking chapattis, but if you do not have one, then make sure you use a heavy-based frying pan as the chapatties need even distribution of heat during cooking. Overheating of the pan will cause the chapatties to stick to the pan and burn.

5. Heat the griddle or frying pan over a medium heat and place a chapatti on it, cook for 30 seconds and turn the chapatti over. Cook until brown spots appear on both sides, turning it over frequently.

6. To keep the chapatties warm, line a piece of aluminium foil with kitchen paper and place the chapatties on one half, cover with the other half and seal the edges.

TIME: Preparation takes 20-25 minutes, cooking takes 35-40 minutes.

SERVING IDEAS: Serve with any meat, chicken or vegetable curry. Suitable for freezing.

LOOCHIS

Loochis are similar to puris – the main difference is that they are made with plain flour.

MAKES 14-15 LOOCHIS

275g/10oz plain flour plus 1 tbsp extra flour for dusting
½ tsp salt
¼ tsp sugar
1 tsp kalonji (onion seeds); optional
15g/½oz butter, margarine or ghee
140-175ml/5-6 fl oz warm water (this will depend on the texture of the flour)
Oil for deep frying

1. In a large bowl, mix the flour, salt, sugar and kalonji. Rub in the fat and gradually add the water. Either knead with your hands or in a food processor until a stiff dough is formed.

2. Divide the dough into 14-15 walnut-sized pieces, and roll each in a circular motion between your palms. Press them down gently to make flat, 1.25cm/½-inch thick round cakes. When you have made all the round cakes, cover them with a damp cloth.

3. Dust each flattened cake lightly with the extra flour and roll out to 9cm/3½-inch discs. It is easier to roll out and fry one loochi at a time unless you have someone to help you. If you roll out all of them first, they need to be kept in a single layer – piling them on top of each other may cause them to stick together.

4. Loochis puff up like balloons during frying. To ensure that the loochis are beautifully puffed, roll them out carefully and evenly without damaging or piercing them. Use a flat perforated spoon for frying.

5. Heat the oil to 160°C/325°F in a deep-fat fryer. Place one loochi at a time in the hot oil – it will soon float to the surface and start puffing up. It helps to cook the loochis evenly if you press it down gently by touching the spoon only to the edge of the loochi. As soon as the loochi puffs up, turn it over gently and cook for about 30 seconds or until lightly browned. Drain on kitchen paper. Fry the rest of the loochis the same way.

6. Keep the fried loochis in a single layer, piling one on top of the other will damage them.

TIME: Preparation takes 10-15 minutes, cooking takes 15-20 minutes.

Mozzarella Pizza

Home-made pizza tastes really delicious and makes excellent party or supper fare.

SERVES 4

Bread Dough
250g/9oz plain flour, sieved
Pinch salt
1 tbsp fast action yeast
120ml/4 fl oz lukewarm water
60ml/2 fl oz milk

Tomato Sauce
2 tbsps olive oil
1 onion, finely chopped
4 large tomatoes, seeded, skinned and crushed
1 bay leaf
1 sprig thyme
A few drops Tabasco sauce
1 clove garlic, crushed
Salt and pepper

Topping
2 tomatoes, sliced
½ onion, finely sliced
2 slices ham, cut into small pieces
200g/7oz Mozzarella cheese, thinly sliced
Salt and pepper
1 tsp marjoram

1. Mix the flour, salt and yeast in a large bowl. Make a well in the centre and add the water and milk.

2. Using a wooden spoon, beat the liquid in the centre of the well, gradually incorporating the flour until it forms a firm dough.

3. Knead the dough on a floured board for 5 minutes or until smooth and elastic. Place in an oiled bowl, cover with a damp tea towel and leave to rise in a warm place for about 30 minutes, or until doubled in bulk.

4. Meanwhile, make the tomato sauce. Heat the oil in a saucepan and add the onion. Sauté until softened, then add the remaining ingredients. Bring to the boil then simmer for about 20 minutes, stirring frequently, or until reduced.

5. Allow the sauce to cool then remove the bay leaf and thyme.

6. Meanwhile, knock back the dough and knead lightly. Flatten the dough and roll out on a floured surface to a 25cm/10-inch circle. Transfer to a baking sheet.

7. Spread the cooled tomato sauce evenly over the dough. Top with the tomato slices, the onion and ham. Lay the mozzarella slices on top, season with salt and pepper and sprinkle over the marjoram.

8. Bake in an oven preheated to 220°C/425°F/Gas Mark 7 for about 15 minutes, or until the cheese is melted and the crust brown and crisp.

TIME: Preparation takes about 1 hour including rising. The pizza takes about 15 minutes to cook.

VARIATIONS: Use any topping ingredients that you fancy, such as pepperoni, olives, peppers, prawns or anchovies.

Banana and Date Loaf

Banana cakes are an ideal way of using up over-ripe bananas, the riper they are, the more flavour they seem to add to the finished cake.

MAKES 1× 900g/2lb LOAF

60ml/4 tbsps milk
1 tbsp treacle
120g/4oz butter or margarine
90g/3oz light muscovado sugar
2 eggs, beaten
175g/6oz self-raising flour, sieved
90g/3oz pitted dates, chopped
1 small ripe banana, peeled and sliced
60g/2oz walnuts, chopped
Glacé icing, walnut halves and banana slices, to decorate

1. Put the milk, treacle, butter and sugar in a saucepan and heat, stirring until the fat melts and the sugar dissolves. Cool slightly then beat in the eggs.

2. Put the flour, dates, banana and nuts in a large bowl and make a well in the centre. Pour the egg and treacle mixture into the centre and beat, gradually incorporating the flour until a thick batter is formed.

3. Pour the batter into a greased and base lined 900g/2lb loaf tin. Bake for 45-50 minutes in the centre of an oven preheated to 190°C/375°F/Gas Mark 5, until a skewer inserted into the centre of the loaf comes out clean. Cool slightly in the tin, before transferring to a wire rack to cool completely.

4. Cover with glacé icing and arrange walnut halves on top. Just before serving arrange banana slices, dipped in lemon juice to prevent discolouring, around the loaf.

TIME: Preparation takes about 15 minutes, cooking takes about 45 minutes.

VARIATION: Use honey in place of the treacle in this recipe.

Spiced Cranberry Nut Teabread

Teabreads don't rely on yeast to make them rise so they are quick and easy to prepare.

MAKES 1 LOAF

225g/8oz plain flour
1 tsp baking powder
225g/8oz sugar
1 tsp baking soda
Pinch salt
¼ tsp ground nutmeg
¼ tsp ground ginger
120ml/4 fl oz orange juice
30g/1oz butter or margarine, melted
60ml/4 tbsps water
1 egg
120g/4oz fresh cranberries, roughly chopped
120g/4oz hazelnuts, roughly chopped

1. Sift the dry ingredients and spices into a large mixing bowl. Make a well in the centre of the dry ingredients and pour in the orange juice, melted butter or margarine, water and egg.

2. Using a wooden spoon, beat the liquid mixture, gradually drawing in the flour from the outside edge. Add the cranberries and nuts and stir to mix.

3. Lightly grease a 23 × 12.5cm/9 × 5 inch loaf tin. Line the base and sides with a greased strip of greaseproof paper, then lightly flour the whole inside of the tin.

4. Spoon or pour in the bread mixture and bake in a preheated 160°C/325°F/Gas Mark 3 oven for about 1 hour, or until a skewer inserted into the centre of the loaf comes out clean.

5. Remove from the tin, carefully peel off the paper and cool on a wire rack. Lightly dust with icing sugar, if wished, and cut into slices to serve.

TIME: Preparation takes about 25 minutes and cooking takes about 1 hour.

WATCHPOINT: Be sure to bake the bread mixture as soon as possible after the baking powder has been added or the bread will not rise the way it should.

SERVING IDEAS: Serve warm or cold with butter or cream cheese with tea or coffee.

FRUIT LOAF

There is no need to add sugar to this recipe as the easy-blend yeast will work on the natural sugars provided by the fruit.

MAKES 2 LOAVES

460g/1lb strong plain flour
½ tsp cinnamon
½ tsp nutmeg
½ tsp salt
1 sachet of easy blend yeast
225g/8oz sultanas
225g/8oz currants
60g/2oz cut mixed peel
2 tbsps vegetable oil
280ml/½ pint lukewarm milk
1 large egg

1. Put the flour, spices, salt and yeast into a large mixing bowl. Stir in the sultanas, currants and mixed peel, mixing well to distribute the fruit evenly.

2. Put the oil, milk and egg into a large jug, and beat together with a fork until the egg is broken up evenly. Add the mixture to the flour, and mix together, stirring until the dough becomes stiff and elastic.

3. Turn the dough onto a lightly floured board, and knead for about 10 minutes or until smooth.

4. Return the dough to the bowl and cover with a damp cloth or a piece of clingfilm. Leave in a warm place for about 1 hour to allow the dough to double in size.

5. Punch the dough down to remove the air, and turn it out onto the lightly floured surface. Knead for about 5 minutes, then cut into two.

6. Shape each piece of dough to fit 2 × 17.5cm/7-inch non-stick loaf tins. Cover each tin lightly with clingfilm or a damp cloth, and leave in a warm place until the loaves have risen to double their size.

7. Bake the loaves for 30-40 minutes in the centre of a preheated oven at 200°C/400°F/ Gas Mark 6. Remove the loaves from the oven after 20 minutes, to brush the surfaces with a little milk.

8. To test if the loaves are cooked, turn out of the tins and tap the bases with your knuckles, if they sound hollow, the loaves are ready. Serve warm, or allow to cool and serve sliced, with butter.

TIME: Preparation takes approximately 2 hours, cooking takes 40 minutes.

VARIATIONS: Use any combination of your favourite dried fruits in this recipe.

TO FREEZE: These loaves freeze well, wrapped tightly in foil, for up to 2 months.

APRICOT AND ALMOND TEABREAD

Good news for those with a sweet tooth, cakes and teabreads are an excellent and delicious way of introducing fibre into the diet, and this recipe is no exception.

MAKES 1 LOAF

175g/6oz butter or margarine
120g/4oz soft brown sugar, or molasses
3 eggs, beaten
225g/8oz wholemeal self-raising flour
2 tbsps milk
120g/4oz dried apricots, chopped
60g/2oz shelled almonds chopped
2 tsps clear honey, warmed
Few extra chopped dried apricots, to decorate

1. Lightly grease a 900g/2lb loaf tin and line the base with a piece of greaseproof paper.

2. Cream together the butter and sugar, until light and fluffy.

3. Beat in the eggs, a little at a time, adding a teaspoonful of flour with each addition, if the mixture shows signs of curdling.

4. Fold in the flour carefully and finally stir in the milk, apricots and nuts.

5. Put the mixture into the prepared loaf tin, smoothing the top level.

6. Bake in a preheated oven at 160°C/325°F/Gas Mark 3, for 1½ hours, or until a skewer inserted into the centre of the loaf comes out clean.

7. As soon as the loaf comes out of the oven, brush the top with the warmed honey and sprinkle with the extra chopped apricots. Leave to cool in the tin for a few minutes, before turning out and leaving to cool completely on a wire rack.

TIME: Preparation takes about 20 minutes, and cooking takes about 1½ hours.

VARIATION: Substitute any favourite dried fruit and nuts for those suggested in this recipe.

TO FREEZE: Wrapped tightly in foil, this teabread will freeze well for up to 2 months.

GINGERBREAD

Dark treacle and fresh ginger combine to make this favourite family cake.

MAKES ONE 17.5cm/7-inch SQUARE CAKE

120g/4oz unsalted butter
120ml/4 fl oz black treacle
225g/8oz light soft brown sugar
120ml/4 fl oz hot water
275g/10oz plain flour
2 tsps baking powder
2 tsps peeled and grated fresh root ginger
1 tsp grated nutmeg
1 egg, beaten

1. Put the butter into a large saucepan, along with the treacle and sugar. Heat gently, stirring all the time, until the sugar and butter have melted together.

2. Pour in the hot water, mix well and set aside.

3. Sift the flour with the baking powder into a large bowl. Make a well in the centre, and add the ginger, nutmeg and beaten egg.

4. Gradually beat in the treacle, using a wooden spoon, slowly drawing the flour from the outside into the centre.

5. Line the base of a 17.5cm/7-inch square cake tin with silicone or lightly greased greaseproof paper.

6. Pour the gingerbread mixture into the cake tin, and bake in a preheated oven at 160°C/325°F/Gas Mark 3, for 1-1½ hours. Test during this time with a skewer; it should come out clean when the cake is cooked.

7. Allow the cake to cool in the tin, before turning out onto a wire rack. Cut into squares to serve.

TIME: Preparation takes about 15 minutes, cooking takes 1-1½ hours.

VARIATION: Add 60g/2oz chopped mixed fruit to the gingerbread mixture along with the spices.

SERVING IDEA: Serve as a dessert with a lemon sauce.

TO FREEZE: This cake freezes well for up to 1 month.

Prune and Walnut Loaf

If you do not have prunes, dates taste just as good.

MAKES 1 LOAF

340g/12oz prunes
175ml/6 fl oz water
340g/12oz fine wholemeal flour
2 tsps baking powder
60g/2oz brown sugar
1 tsp mixed spice
120g/4oz walnuts, chopped
60ml/4 tbsps sunflower oil
1 egg
Orange juice
Whole walnuts to decorate

1. Simmer the prunes in the water until soft. Allow to cool and retain the cooking liquid. Remove the stones and chop the prunes finely.

2. Mix the flour, baking powder, sugar, spice and walnuts together.

3. In a separate bowl mix the prunes, cooking liquid, oil and egg.

4. Fold together the flour mixture and the prune mixture, adding enough orange juice to give a soft consistency.

5. Put into a greased and lined 900g/2lb loaf tin and decorate with walnuts.

6. Bake in an oven preheated to 160°C/325°F/Gas Mark 3, for 1¼ hours or until a skewer inserted into the centre of the loaf comes out clean.

TIME: Preparation takes 15 minutes, cooking takes 1¼ hours.

TO FREEZE: Freeze after cooking, for up to 2 months, wrapped tightly in foil.

Banana Loaf

Eat this on its own as a cake, or slice thinly and butter to serve for elevenses or afternoon tea.

MAKES 1 LOAF

1 tea cup of porridge oats
1 tea cup of sugar
1 tea cup of mixed fruit
1 tea cup of Granose banana-flavoured soya milk
1 breakfast cup of self-raising flour
Pinch of nutmeg

1. Begin preparing the cake the day before it is to be cooked. Place all the ingredients except the self-raising flour and nutmeg into a large bowl and stir well.

2. Cover and put into the refrigerator overnight.

3. The following day, line or grease a 460g/1lb loaf tin.

4. Mix the self-raising flour and the nutmeg gently into the mixture and put into the loaf tin.

5. Bake in an oven preheated to 180°C/350°F/ Gas Mark 4, for an hour or until a skewer inserted into the loaf comes out clean.

TIME: Preparation takes 10 minutes, cooking takes 1 hour.

VARIATIONS: ½ tsp of mixed spice may be used in place of the nutmeg. Ordinary milk or plain soya milk can be used instead of banana soya milk.

SERVING IDEA: Eat on its own as a cake, or slice thinly and butter to serve for elevenses or afternoon tea.

COOK'S TIP: The loaf becomes more moist if left in an airtight tin for a day or two before eating.

Apple Bread

Adding molasses to this teabread not only gives it a good flavour, but also makes it almost black.

MAKES 1 LOAF

1 tsp bicarbonate of soda
60ml/4 tbsps buttermilk
150g/5oz freshly grated apple
340g/12oz molasses
1 tsp cinnamon
½ tsp cloves
½ tsp allspice
¼ tsp salt
Plain flour

1. Dissolve the bicarbonate of soda in the buttermilk. Combine this with all the other ingredients, adding enough flour to make a stiff mixture.

2. Turn into a greased loaf tin and bake in an oven preheated to 180°C/350°F/Gas Mark 4, for 1-1¼ hours, or until a skewer inserted into the middle of the bread comes out clean.

3. Leave in the tin to cool slightly, then turn out onto a cake rack to cool completely. Eat as fresh as possible.

TIME: Preparation takes about 15 minutes and cooking takes 1-1¼ hours.

COOK'S TIP: Eat this teabread as fresh as possible, serve sliced and buttered.

Succulent Scones

These scones make an ideal accompaniment for soup in place of bread.

MAKES 6-8 SCONES

225g/8oz wholemeal flour
225g/8oz white flour
1 scant tsp salt
1 scant tsp bicarbonate of soda
1 scant tsp cream of tartar
60g/2oz unsalted butter
140ml/¼ pint natural yogurt
Milk
1 egg, well beaten

1. Sift the flours, salt, soda and cream of tartar twice into a mixing bowl and rub in the butter.

2. Put the yogurt into a measuring jug and make up to 280ml/½ pint with milk; stir well.

3. Quickly stir the beaten egg into the flour followed by the yogurt and milk.

4. When the mixture has formed a soft dough, knead lightly for a few seconds.

5. Divide the dough into 6 or 8 pieces and form into circles on an oiled baking sheet.

6. Flatten the dough with your fingers and prick with a fork.

7. Bake in an oven preheated to 220°C/425°F/Gas Mark 7, for 8-10 minutes or until just coloured.

TIME: Preparation takes about 15 minutes, cooking takes 8-10 minutes.

VARIATION: Add 60g/2oz of presoaked raisins or sultanas and serve for afternoon tea.

Wholemeal Muffins

These muffins can be served as a sweet or savoury treat.

MAKES 24

225g/8oz wholemeal flour
60g/2oz plain flour
1 tsp bicarbonate of soda
225ml/8 fl oz milk
140ml/4 fl oz buttermilk
30g/1oz butter, melted
2 tbsps molasses

1. Sift all the dry ingredients together into a bowl.

2. Make a well in the centre and add the milk and buttermilk. Gradually incorporate the flour, and beat well to obtain a smooth mixture.

3. Stir in the melted butter and the molasses.

4. Divide the mixture between two greased 12-space muffins tins.

5. Bake in a preheated 220°C/425°F/Gas Mark 7 oven, for about 20 minutes, or until brown.

TIME: Preparation takes about 15 minutes and cooking takes 20 minutes.

SERVING IDEA: Serve with butter and apricot jam, or cream cheese and chives.

Saffron Teacakes

Saffron adds flavour as well as colour to these delicious buns.

MAKES 10-12 TEACAKES

140ml/¼ pint milk
Good pinch saffron strands
225g/8oz self-raising flour
120g/4oz unsalted butter
120g/4oz currants
½ tsp allspice
30g/1oz candied peel
60g/2oz caster sugar
1 egg, beaten

1. Heat 60ml/4 tbsps of the milk in a small saucepan and add the saffron. Allow to stand for 10-15 minutes to infuse.

2. Sift the flour into a large bowl and rub in the butter, until it resembles fine breadcrumbs.

3. Stir the currants, allspice, peel and sugar into the flour and butter mixture.

4. Make a well in the centre of the flour and stir in the saffron milk and the remainder of the milk. Mix well to form a soft dough.

5. Turn the dough onto a lightly floured board, and knead until smooth.

6. Roll the dough into a circle approximately 1.25cm/½-inch thick. Cut into 10-12 rounds with a 7.5cm/3-inch pastry cutter.

7. Arrange the individual rounds on a lightly greased baking sheet, and brush the top with a little beaten egg.

8. Bake the cakes in a preheated oven at 180°C/350°F/Gas Mark 4, for 20-30 minutes, until they are well risen and golden brown.

TIME: Preparation takes 15 minutes, cooking will take 20-30 minutes.

COOK'S TIP: Do not be tempted to use too much saffron; a little will go a very long way.

TO FREEZE: These teacakes freeze very well for up to 1 month.

Lemon and Raisin Drop Scones

Cooked rice is the surprise ingredient in these cakes that are crisp outside, yet soft and light inside.

MAKES 24

120g/4oz long-grain rice
120g/4oz plain flour
1 tsp baking powder
Pinch salt
120g/4oz sugar
2 eggs, separated
90ml/6 tbsps milk
Grated rind of 1 lemon
45g/4 tbsps raisins

1. Cook the rice in boiling water for 15-20 minutes or until tender. Rinse, drain and leave to cool completely.

2. Sift the flour, baking powder and salt into a mixing bowl and stir in the sugar.

3. Beat the yolks with the milk and add gradually to the dry ingredients, stirring constantly, to make a thick batter. Stir in the rice.

4. Beat the egg whites until stiff but not dry and fold into the batter along with the lemon rind and raisins.

5. Lightly oil a heavy frying pan and place over a moderate heat. When the pan is hot, drop in 4-6 separate tablespoons of batter and if necessary, spread into small circles with the back of the spoon.

6. Cook until brown on the underside and bubbles form on the top surface. Turn over and cook the other side.

7. Repeat until all the batter is used, keeping the cakes warm. Serve plain or buttered.

TIME: Preparation takes about 40 minutes and cooking takes about 40-45 minutes.

COOK'S TIP: To drain rice thoroughly, place in a colander and make several drainage holes with the handle of a wooden spoon.

SERVING IDEAS: Squeeze lemon juice over the hot scones, or spoon on jam. These can also be served cold.

Sticky Buns

Serve these buns warm for a tea-time treat.

MAKES 12

60ml/4 tbsps warm water
½oz fresh yeast
225ml/8 fl oz lukewarm milk
½ tsp salt
340g/12oz flour
Brown sugar
60g/2oz butter, softened
1 tsp cinnamon
90g/3oz raisins
3 tbsps chopped candied peel
60g/2oz chopped pecans

1. Combine the water and yeast, and leave to stand for 5 minutes or until frothy. Stir in the milk.

2. Combine the salt, flour and 1 teaspoon brown sugar in a large bowl. Make a well in the centre of the dry ingredients and pour in the yeast mixture. Mix to a soft dough.

3. Knead the dough for about 10 minutes on a floured surface. When it is smooth and elastic, place the dough in an oiled bowl and cover with a damp tea-towel.

4. Stand the bowl in a warm place and leave for about 2 hours, or until the dough triples in size.

5. Knock the air out of the dough and knead again a few minutes. Roll out the dough to a rectangle about 5mm/¼-inch thick.

6. Spread over the butter and sprinkle with the cinnamon, raisins, candied peel and about 1 tablespoon brown sugar. Roll up like a swiss roll and cut into 2cm/¾ inch-thick slices.

7. Place the slices close together in a lightly buttered baking tin. Allow to rise again for about 20 minutes.

8. Sprinkle the top liberally with brown sugar and scatter over the pecans. Bake in a pre-heated 200°C/400°F/Gas Mark 6 oven, for about 20-25 minutes. Cool slightly in the tin before removing to a wire rack.

TIME: Preparation takes about 40 minutes plus about 2 hours 20 minutes proving time. Cooking takes 20-25 minutes.

COOK'S TIP: If wished, use 1 tbsp dried active yeast – add directly to the flour and stir in the water.

CRUMPETS

Crumpets are wonderful for afternoon tea on a cold winter's day.

MAKES ABOUT 12

280ml/½ pint milk
60ml/4 tbsps water
1 tsp caster sugar
1 tbsp dried yeast
225g/8oz strong plain flour
1 tsp salt

1. Heat the milk and water together in a small saucepan until lukewarm.

2. Transfer to a jug and stir in the sugar and dried yeast. Leave in a warm place until frothy.

3. Meanwhile, sift the flour and salt into a mixing bowl, make a well in the centre and, when it is ready, pour in the yeast mixture.

4. Gradually incorporate the dry ingredients with a wooden spoon, beating to a smooth batter. Cover the bowl with a tea-towel and leave to stand for 45 minutes.

5. Grease a heavy-based frying pan and the insides of some crumpet rings.

6. When the pan is hot, spoon a tablespoon of batter into each ring. After about 5 minutes the traditional holes will appear.

7. Lift off the rings and turn the crumpets over carefully. Cook for a further minute. Repeat this process until all the batter is used up.

TIME: Preparation takes about 15 minutes and cooking takes 6 minutes per batch.

BUYING GUIDE: Crumpet rings are available in specialist kitchen shops. Large plain metal pastry cutters will work also.

SERVING IDEAS: Serve warm with butter and jam. Best toasted to reheat.

Oatmeal and Treacle Scones

A tasty alternative to plain scones.

MAKES ABOUT 12 SCONES

120g/4oz plain wholemeal flour
2 level tsps baking powder
Pinch of salt
30g/1oz butter or margarine
120g/4oz oatmeal
1 tbsp molasses
Milk to bind

1. Sieve the flour, baking powder and salt into a bowl three times, to aerate it.

2. Rub in the butter, then add the oatmeal.

3. Warm the molasses and 1 tbsp of milk.

4. Bind the flour mixture with the molasses and milk, adding extra milk as necessary.

5. Roll out to 5mm/¼-inch thick and cut into 5cm/2-inch rounds.

6. Bake on a greased baking sheet in an oven preheated to 220°C/425°F/Gas Mark 7, for 10 minutes.

7. Remove and place on a wire rack to cool.

TIME: Preparation takes 10 minutes, cooking takes 10 minutes.

TO FREEZE: The scones may be placed in a freezer bag or container and frozen after cooking.

Strawberry Shortcakes

Summer wouldn't be the same without a delicious strawberry dessert. The scone-like cakes can be made in advance.

SERVES 6

225g/8oz plain flour
1 tbsp baking powder
Pinch salt
3 tbsps sugar
90g/3oz cream cheese, softened
45g/1½oz butter or margarine
1 egg, beaten
90-120ml/3-4 fl oz milk
Melted butter
460g/1lb fresh or frozen strawberries
Juice of ½ orange
Icing sugar
280ml/½ pint whipped cream

1. Sift the flour, baking powder, salt and sugar into a large bowl.

2. Using 2 knives or forks, cut in the cheese and butter or margarine. A food processor can also be used for this.

3. Blend in the egg and enough milk to make a firm dough.

4. Knead lightly on a floured surface and then roll out to a thickness of 1.25cm/½-inch.

5. Cut the dough into an even number of 75cm/3-inch circles. Re-roll the trimmings and cut as before. Brush half of the circles with some melted butter and place the other halves on top, pressing down lightly.

6. Bake on an ungreased baking sheet for about 15 minutes in a pre-heated 220°C/425°F/Gas Mark 7 oven. Allow to cool slightly and then transfer to a wire rack.

7. Hull the strawberries and wash well. Purée half of them in a food processor or blender with the orange juice, adding icing sugar to taste if wished. Cut the remaining strawberries in half and combine with the purée.

8. Separate the shortcakes in half and place the bottoms on serving plates. Spoon over the strawberries and sauce and pipe or spoon on the cream.

9. Sprinkle the tops of the shortcakes with icing sugar and place on top of the cream. Serve slightly warm or at room temperature.

TIME: Preparation takes about 30-35 minutes and cooking takes about 15 minutes.

VARIATION: Other fruit may be used to fill the shortcakes. Substitute peaches, apricots or other berries.

Griddle Scones

The whole fun of these cakes is that they can be eaten directly from the pan in which they are cooked. So gather family and friends around you for a traditional tea-time treat.

SERVES 4-6

120g/4oz self-raising flour
Pinch salt
45g/1½oz butter or margarine
120g/4oz currants
½ tsp ground nutmeg
1 egg
90ml/3 fl oz milk

1. Mix the flour and salt together, and rub in the butter until the mixture resembles fine breadcrumbs. Stir in the currants and the nutmeg.

2. Beat together the egg and the milk. Make a well in the centre of the flour and pour in the liquid.

3. Using a wooden spoon, mix the egg and milk mixture into the flour, stirring from the centre of the bowl and drawing the flour in from the sides to form a smooth, thick batter.

4. Heat a heavy-based griddle or a frying pan over a moderate heat, and grease with a little butter or oil.

5. Drop tablespoons of the batter into the hot pan, and cook for 2-3 minutes, or until the bases are set and have turned golden brown.

6. Turn the scones over and cook on the other side in the same way.

7. Serve from the griddle with jam and cream.

TIME: Preparation takes 15 minutes, cooking takes about 4 minutes per batch of scones.

PREPARATION: If the batter is too thick, add a little extra milk until it becomes a soft dropping consistency.

TO FREEZE: These scones freeze well, and can be re-heated in a warm oven, under a grill or in a toaster.

Cornmeal Muffins

A cross between cake and bread, these muffins are slightly sweet and crumbly. They are nice with butter or jam as a tea time treat, or serve as you would hot rolls.

MAKES 12

120g/4oz plain flour
60g/4 tbsps sugar
2 tsps baking powder
½ tsp salt
150g/5oz yellow cornmeal
1 egg, slightly beaten
60ml/4 tbsps oil
300ml/11 fl oz milk

1. Grease a 12-space patty tin liberally with oil. Heat the tin for 5 minutes in an oven preheated to 230°C/450°F/Gas Mark 8.

2. Meanwhile, sift the flour, sugar, baking powder and salt into a large bowl. Add the cornmeal and stir to blend, leaving a well in the centre.

3. Combine the egg, oil and milk and pour into the well.

4. Beat with a wooden spoon, gradually incorporating the dry ingredients into the liquid. Do not overbeat the mixture. It can be slightly lumpy.

5. Spoon the batter into the hot tin and bake for about 14 minutes.

6. Cool briefly in the tin and then remove to a wire rack to cool further. Serve warm.

TIME: Preparation takes about 20 minutes and cooking takes about 14 minutes.

VARIATION: If you have a cast iron frying pan, coat liberally with oil and place in the oven to pre-heat. Pour the batter into the pan and then bake. Cut into wedges and serve directly from the pan.

TO FREEZE: Cornmeal muffins may be baked and frozen, well wrapped, for up to 2 months. Defrost at room temperature and reheat wrapped in foil for about 5 minutes in a moderate oven. Do not overheat as the muffins can dry out easily.

Cheese and Paprika Scones

These moreish savoury scones are best eaten warm the same day they are made.

MAKES 10

225g/8oz self-raising flour, sieved
1 tsp paprika
Pinch salt
60g/2oz butter or margarine
60g/2oz red leicester cheese, grated
1 tsp English mustard
1 egg
60ml/4 tbsps milk
1 tsp Marmite or yeast extract
Little boiling water

1. Place the flour, paprika and salt in a mixing bowl and rub in the butter until the mixture resembles fine breadcrumbs. Stir in the cheese.

2. Beat the mustard, egg and milk together in a small bowl and pour into the flour and cheese. Mix well to form a soft dough adding a little extra milk if necessary.

3. Roll out the dough to about 1cm/½-inch thick and cut into 10 rounds with a 5cm/2-inch plain cutter. Place on a lightly greased baking sheet.

4. Mix the marmite or yeast extract with a little boiling water and brush over the tops of the scones. Bake for 10-15 minutes in an oven preheated to 200°C/400°F/Gas Mark 6 or until risen and golden. Transfer to a wire rack to cool.

TIME: Preparation takes about 20 minutes, cooking time is about 15 minutes.

VARIATIONS: Omit the yeast extract and brush the scones with a little milk, then sprinkle with sesame seeds and a little extra cheese.

PREPARATION: Use 90ml/6 tbsps natural yogurt instead of the egg in this recipe if preferred.

Buttermilk Muffins

These American muffins are quite different to English ones, but just as tasty.

MAKES 12

120g/4oz plain flour
½ tsp salt
½ tsp bicarbonate of soda
225ml/8 fl oz buttermilk
15g/½oz butter, melted

1. Lightly butter a 12-space muffin or deep patty tin.

2. Beat all the ingredients together thoroughly and divide equally between the tins.

3. Bake in an oven preheated to 220°C/425°F/Gas Mark 7, for about 20 minutes, until the muffins are well browned.

TIME: Preparation takes about 10 minutes and cooking takes about 20 minutes.

COOK'S TIP: Eat these muffins as fresh as possible.

Scotch Pancakes

Scotch pancakes or drop scones as they are also called, are delicious eaten with butter and jam or golden syrup.

MAKES ABOUT 24

225g/8oz plain flour
2 tsps cream of tartar
1 tsp bicarbonate of soda
½ tsp salt
30g/1oz caster sugar
Approximately 175ml/6 fl oz milk
1 egg, beaten
2 tsps golden syrup

1. Set a griddle, or heavy-based frying pan over a medium heat.

2. Meanwhile, sift together the flour, cream of tartar, bicarbonate of soda and the salt into a bowl. Stir in the sugar.

3. Make a well in the centre and gradually add the milk, beaten egg and syrup until a smooth pouring batter is formed (it must not be too thin).

4. Grease the cooking surface lightly with a little oil and, when a slight haze appears, pour on dessertspoons of the batter, a few at a time, leaving plenty of space between each one.

5. When bubbles appear on the surface and the undersides are brown, flip them over with a palette knife. Cook a little longer until the second sides are pale golden. Serve at once.

TIME: Preparation takes about 10 minutes and cooking takes about 15-20 minutes altogether.

COOK'S TIP: Scotch pancakes freeze very well and can be reheated in a hot oven, under a grill, or in a toaster.

PREPARATION: If you want nice round scotch pancakes, set large plain well greased metal pastry cutters on to the griddle and pour the batter into them. Remove rings once the pancakes have set. Clean and re-grease before using again.

Fruit Scones

Scones are always a firm favourite and do not need any added sugar when made with plenty of fruit.

MAKES 10-12

225g/8oz plain flour
1 tsp cream of tartar
½ tsp bicarbonate of soda
¼ tsp salt
45g/1½oz butter
90g/3oz sultanas
15g/½oz sunflower seeds
15g/½oz fresh root ginger
2 eggs
Extra milk for blending
Beaten egg, for glaze

1. Mix the flour, cream of tartar, bicarbonate of soda and salt together, and sieve it twice through a metal sieve to aerate completely.

2. Put the sieved flour into a large bowl and rub in the butter until the mixture resembles fine breadcrumbs.

3. Stir the sultanas and the sunflower seeds into the flour and butter mixture.

4. Peel the ginger and cut, or grate, it into very small pieces. Using a pestle and mortar or the blade of a large knife, crush the ginger until it becomes a paste.

5. Put the ginger into a small bowl along with the eggs, and beat together with a fork until they are evenly blended.

6. Add the beaten eggs and ginger to the flour and sultana mixture, mixing well to form a soft dough, and adding a little extra milk if the dough is too stiff.

7. Lightly flour a work surface. Turn out the dough and knead it lightly until it becomes smooth.

8. Roll the dough out to approximately 1.25cm/½-inch thick and cut it into 5cm/2-inch rounds using a pastry cutter.

9. Place the scones on a greased baking sheet, and brush each one with the extra beaten egg. Bake in a pre-heated oven at 200°C/400°F/Gas Mark 6 for 10-15 minutes or until golden brown and well risen.

TIME: Preparation takes about 15 minutes, cooking takes 10-15 minutes.

PREPARATION: Do not roll the dough out too thinly, otherwise the scones will not rise properly.

VARIATION: Use other combinations of dried fruit and nuts, or seeds, in place of the sultanas and sunflower seeds in this recipe.

Yogurt Scones

Serve with jam and cream.

MAKES 10 SCONES

60g/2oz butter or margarine
225g/8oz wholemeal self-raising flour
30g/1oz demerara sugar
60g/1oz raisins
Plain yogurt to mix

1. Rub the fat into the flour and sugar. Stir in the raisins and mix well.

2. Add enough yogurt to mix to a fairly stiff dough.

3. Turn the mixture out onto a floured board and knead lightly. Make two large circles of dough or cut into 2.5cm/2-inch rounds.

4. Bake in a preheated oven for 15-17 minutes at 210°C/425°F/Gas Mark 7.

5. Remove and cool on a wire rack.

TIME: Preparation takes 10 minutes, cooking takes 15-17 minutes.

VARIATIONS: Use chopped dried apricots instead of raisins.

Carrot Cake

Carrots give a cake a delicious sweet flavour, as well as lots of vitamins and minerals. What better excuse do you need to indulge in this delicious tea-time treat.

MAKES 1 LOAF

175g/6oz butter
175g/6oz soft brown sugar
2 eggs, well beaten
225g/8oz plain wholemeal flour
1½ tsps bicarbonate of soda
½ tsp baking powder
¼ tsp ground cinnamon
¼ tsp ground nutmeg
¼ tsp cardamom seeds, crushed
½ tsp salt
225g/8oz peeled carrots, grated
90g/3oz raisins
60g/2oz walnuts, finely chopped
Icing sugar, for dredging

1. Cream the butter and sugar together until they are light and fluffy.

2. Add the eggs a little at a time, beating well and adding a teaspoonful of the flour with each addition, to prevent the mixture from curdling.

3. Put the remaining flour into a large bowl along with the bicarbonate of soda, baking powder, cinnamon, nutmeg, cardamom seed and salt. Mix together well.

4. Carefully fold the flour into the butter and egg mixture, mixing well to ensure that it is blended evenly.

5. Stir in the carrots, raisins and nuts to blend evenly.

6. Lightly grease a 25cm/10-inch loaf tin and line the base with a piece of silicone paper.

7. Pour the cake mixture into the loaf tin, and bake in a preheated oven at 180°C/350°F/Gas Mark 4, for 45-50 minutes or until a fine metal skewer comes out clean when inserted into the centre of the cake.

8. Cool the cake in the tin for 15 minutes before turning out onto a wire rack to cool completely.

9. Dredge the cake with icing sugar just before serving.

TIME: Preparation takes 30 minutes, cooking takes 45-50 minutes.

WATCHPOINT: If the egg and butter mixture should curdle, add a little more flour and beat very hard with an electric whisk until the curdling disappears.

TREACLE TART

An old-fashioned favourite. Good served with custard or cream.

SERVES 4-6

225g/8oz shortcrust pastry
175g/8 tbsps golden syrup
2 tbsps lemon juice
60g/2oz fresh white breadcrumbs

1. Roll out the pastry and line a 20cm/8-inch shallow pie dish. Reserve any trimmings.

2. In a small pan, warm the syrup and lemon juice, add the breadcrumbs and pour over pastry base.

3. Roll out the pastry trimmings and cut into thin strips. Use these to make a lattice pattern over the syrup filling.

4. Dampen the ends of the strips and press them lightly onto the edge of the tart.

5. Bake in the centre of an oven preheated to 190°C/375°F/Gas Mark 5, for 25-30 minutes, until the pastry is cooked and the filling golden and firm.

TIME: Preparation takes 25 minutes and cooking takes 25-30 minutes.

VARIATION: A little ground ginger can be added to the filling for extra flavour.

PREPARATION: See Lemon Sponge Pie for pastry recipe and method.

Quiche Lorraine

The history of this French egg and bacon flan goes back to the 16th century in the Lorraine region. Traditionally it doesn't contain cheese, but it's a tasty addition.

SERVES 6

Pâte Brisée

175g/6oz plain flour, sifted
Pinch salt
120g/4oz butter
1 egg
2 tsps iced water

Filling

6 rashers smoked streaky bacon, cut into large dice
1 tsp butter
2 shallots, finely chopped
2 eggs plus 2 egg yolks
280ml/½ pint double cream
Salt, pepper and grated nutmeg
90g/3oz grated Gruyère cheese (optional)

1. To prepare the pastry, sift the flour and salt into a large bowl. Rub in the butter until the mixture looks like fine breadcrumbs – this may also be done in a food processor.

2. Beat the egg lightly and mix into the flour by hand or with the machine. If the dough seems crumbly, add some of the water. Chill well before using.

3. Roll the pastry out to a circle about 5mm/¼-inch thick on a well-floured surface. Roll the pastry over a rolling pin and unroll it onto a 20-22.5cm/8-9 inch flan ring.

4. Gently press the pastry into the bottom and up the sides of the dish, being careful not to stretch it. Trim off the excess pastry and prick the bottom lightly with a fork.

5. Place a circle of greaseproof paper on top of the pastry and fill with dry beans, or rice. Bake for about 10 minutes in an oven preheated to 190°C/375°F/Gas Mark 5, then remove the paper and beans.

6. Prick base again lightly and return to the oven for another 3 minutes or until just beginning to brown. Allow the pastry to cool while preparing the filling.

7. Put the bacon in a small frying pan and fry over a gentle heat until the fat begins to run. Raise the heat and cook until lightly browned and crisp.

8. Place the bacon on kitchen paper to drain and add the butter to the pan if insufficient fat is left. Add the chopped shallots and cook until just beginning to colour. Remove to kitchen paper to drain with the bacon.

9. Beat the eggs and extra yolks, cream and seasonings together in a large bowl.

10. Scatter the bacon and shallots over the bottom of the pastry case and ladle the custard filling on top of it. If using cheese, add with the custard.

11. Bake in the top half of the oven for about 25 minutes, or until the custard has puffed and browned and a knife inserted into the centre comes out clean.

12. Allow to cool slightly and then remove from the ring.

TIME: Preparation takes about 25 minutes, plus time for chilling the pastry. Cooking takes about 40 minutes.

Dutch Pancake

This pancake is more like a Yorkshire pudding than a pancake, although it tastes great with a fruit accompaniment.

SERVES 3-4

60g/2oz flour
Pinch of salt
3 eggs, beaten
120ml/4 fl oz milk

1. Sift the flour into a bowl along with the salt. Make a well in the centre of the flour and add the eggs and milk.

2. Beat with a wooden spoon, gradually mixing in the flour from the outside until a smooth batter is formed.

3. Pour into a large, round buttered cake tin.

4. Place the pancake in an oven preheated to 200°C/400°F/Gas Mark 6, and bake for about 25 minutes, or until well risen and golden brown.

TIME: Preparation takes about 10 minutes and cooking takes about 25 minutes.

SERVING IDEAS: Serve sprinkled with icing sugar and accompany with lemon or orange wedges to squeeze over the top.

SAFFRON BABAS

A baba is a traditional Polish Easter cake. Cooks spoke in whispers when these cakes were cooling since loud noise was believed to damage their delicate texture!

MAKES 2 CAKES

420ml/¾ pint lukewarm milk
90g/3oz fresh yeast
275g/10oz plain flour
175g/6oz sugar
8 egg yolks
4 egg whites
Rind of 1 lemon
3 tbsps brandy
Pinch saffron powder
900g/2lbs plain flour
Pinch salt
175g/6oz melted butter, slightly cooled
120g/4oz raisins
2 tbsps mixed peel

1. Combine the milk and yeast and pour into a well in the centre of the first measure of flour. Mix with a wooden spoon and cover the bowl.

2. Leave in a warm place for about 1 hour, covered with a damp cloth or clingfilm, until it doubles in bulk and the top becomes bubbly.

3. Combine the sugar, egg yolks, egg whites, lemon rind, brandy and saffron. Stir into the yeast mixture and add the remaining flour and salt. Knead the dough by hand for about 30 minutes in the bowl or on a very well-floured surface.

4. Place the dough back in the bowl and add the butter, raisins and peel. Knead the dough by hand until it is smooth and elastic and does not stick. Divide into 2 equal portions.

5. Butter two 25cm/10-inch round cake tins very thickly and place in the dough, patting out evenly. Cover with lightly-oiled clingfilm and put in a warm place to rise until it fills the tins.

6. Bake in a pre-heated 200°C/400°F/Gas Mark 6 oven for about 1 hour. Test with a metal skewer – if the skewer comes out clean when inserted into the centre of the babas the cakes are done.

7. Leave to cool in the tins for about 10-14 minutes and then remove to a cooling rack. Sprinkle with sugar or drizzle with icing.

TIME: Preparation takes about 2 hours, cooking takes about 1 hour.

WATCHPOINT: Do not mix the yeast with milk that is too hot. This can kill the yeast and the cakes will not rise as they should.

Rhubarb Tart

An ideal dessert to make when rhubarb is plentiful. The juice which is left over makes a refreshing drink when diluted with chilled soda water.

SERVES 8

900g/2lbs rhubarb, cut into 2.5cm/1-inch pieces
540g/1lb 3oz caster sugar
120g/4oz butter or margarine
3 eggs
2 tbsps white wine
250g/9oz plain flour
2 tsps baking powder
140ml/¼ pint soured cream
1 tsp ground cinnamon
60g/2oz ground almonds
Icing sugar, to decorate

1. Put the rhubarb into a bowl and sprinkle with 400g/14oz of the sugar. Cover and allow to stand for 1-2 hours.

2. Cream the butter with 90g/3oz of the remaining sugar, until it is light and fluffy.

3. Beat one of the eggs and add this and the wine to the creamed butter and sugar. Sift in the flour and baking powder and mix together well.

4. Lightly knead the base mixture together until it forms a smooth dough. Wrap the dough in greaseproof paper and chill for 30 minutes in the refrigerator.

5. Roll out the dough on a lightly floured board and use it to line a well-greased, loose-based, or spring-clip, 25cm/10-inch round, deep flan tin, pressing the pastry well into the base and up the sides of the tin.

6. Strain the rhubarb and arrange the pieces in the pastry case. Bake in an oven preheated to 180°C/350°F/Gas Mark 4, for 30 minutes.

7. Beat together the cream and the remaining eggs and sugar. Stir in the cinnamon and ground almonds, mixing well to ensure they are thoroughly blended.

8. Remove the flan from the oven and pour the cream topping over the rhubarb. Return the flan to the oven and cook at the same temperature for a further 20-25 minutes, or until the topping is golden brown.

9. Ease the flan out of the tin and cool completely before dusting with icing sugar and serving.

TIME: Preparation takes about 30 minutes, plus 1-2 hours standing time for the rhubarb. Cooking takes 30 minutes for the base, followed by 20-25 minutes for the topping.

VARIATION: Use 900g/2lbs stoned and quartered red plums instead of the rhubarb.

SERVING IDEAS: Serve with whipped double cream.

Apple Strudel

Making strudel used to be something only a skilled cook or baker would tackle. But since ready made filo pastry has become widely available it makes the preparation of such delicious pastries simple.

SERVES 6-8

460g/1lb sliced tart apples
60g/2oz raisins
2 tsps grated lemon rind
90g/3oz sugar
1 tsp cinnamon
45g/1½oz ground almonds
5 large sheets filo pastry
30g/1oz fresh fine breadcrumbs
200g/7oz butter or margarine, melted

1. Mix the apples with the raisins, lemon rind, sugar, cinnamon and almonds. Set aside.

2. Place one sheet of filo pastry on a clean tea-towel and brush with some of the melted butter. Place a second sheet on top and brush with butter again. Repeat until all the sheets have been used, using about 60g/2oz of butter.

3. Cook and stir the breadcrumbs with 30g/1oz of the remaining butter, until lightly browned. Reserve 1 tbsp of crumbs, and sprinkle the remainder on the layered filo pastry.

4. Mound the filling in a 7.5cm/3-inch strip along the narrow edge of the filo, leaving a 5cm/2-inch border. Lift the towel, using it to help roll the filo over the apples, swiss-roll fashion.

5. Brush the strudel with butter after each turn. Using the towel, place the strudel onto a greased baking sheet.

6. Brush the top of the strudel with butter and sprinkle with the reserved crumbs. Bake the strudel in an oven preheated to 200°C/400°F/Gas Mark 6, for 20-25 minutes, or until golden brown. Serve warm.

TIME: Preparation takes about 30 minutes and cooking takes 20-25 minutes.

WATCHPOINT: When using filo pastry it is important to keep it damp. If the pastry drys out it will become brittle.

VARIATIONS: Filo pastry is available in most large supermarkets frozen. Defrost before using.

Lemon Sponge Pie

This delicious pie could also be made with oranges.

SERVES 6-8

Pastry
175g/6oz plain flour
Pinch salt
120g/4oz butter
Iced water

Lemon Sponge Filling
225g/8oz sugar
2 eggs, separated
Juice and rind of 1 lemon
15g/½oz butter, melted
3 tbsps flour
225ml/8 fl oz milk
Lemon slices to decorate
Icing sugar

1. Sieve the flour and salt into a bowl. Rub in the butter, until the mixture resembles bread crumbs, then stir in enough iced water to make a firm dough.

2. Roll the pastry out, on a floured board, to a circle large enough to line the base and sides of a 25.5cm/10-inch pie dish. Chill the pastry case for 30 minutes before filling.

3. Whisk the sugar and egg yolks together until thick and pale lemon in colour. Stir in the lemon juice, rind, butter and flour. Add the milk and mix well.

4. Whisk the egg whites until stiff peaks form, and fold into the lemon mixture.

5. Pour into the pastry case and bake in an oven preheated to 180°C/350°F/Gas Mark 4, for about 50 minutes, or until the filling is puffed and set and pastry is golden.

6. Allow to cool, then decorate with lemon slices and dust with icing sugar.

TIME: Preparation takes 30 minutes plus 30 minutes chilling time. Cooking takes about 50 minutes.

PREPARATION: If the pastry is too soft to roll out, chill before lining the pie dish as well as before filling it.

Victoria Sandwich Cake

A favourite for afternoon tea.

120g/4oz butter or margarine
120g/4oz caster sugar
2 large eggs
Few drops vanilla essence
120g/4oz self-raising flour, sieved

To finish
Jam, whipped cream, sifted icing sugar

1. Grease two 18cm/7-inch straight-sided sandwich tins and line the bases with buttered greaseproof paper.

2. In a medium-sized mixing bowl, cream together the butter and sugar until light and fluffy. Beat in the eggs one at a time and add the vanilla essence.

3. With a metal spoon, gently fold in the sifted flour. When it is all incorporated, divide the mixture equally between the two tins, levelling off the surface.

4. Bake on the centre shelf of an oven preheated to 180°C/350°F/Gas Mark 4, for about 25 minutes or until risen and springy to the touch.

5. Leave to cool for a minute in the tins, then turn out onto wire cooling racks. Carefully peel off the greaseproof paper.

6. When cold, sandwich together with jam and whipped cream and dust the top with sifted icing sugar.

TIME: Preparation takes about 15 minutes and cooking takes 25 minutes.

COOK'S TIP: Test to see if the cake is cooked by gently pressing the centre of the sponge with a finger. The cake should feel springy and your finger should leave no impression.

Almond Tart

This delicious almond tart could be served with a custard sauce as a dessert.

SERVES 8-10

175g/6oz frozen puff pastry
120g/4oz butter or margarine
120g/4oz caster sugar
2 eggs
120g/4oz self-raising flour
½ tsp almond essence
1 egg-cup of milk
Damson jam
60g/2oz grated marzipan (left uncovered in the refrigerator to harden before grating)

1. Take 120g/4oz of the puff pastry, roll it out thinly and use to line a greased 25cm/10-inch flan tin.

2. Roll out the remainder of the pastry slightly thicker, cut into strips 1.25cm/½-inch wide and set aside.

3. Slightly soften the butter, then cream with the sugar. Add one of the eggs, beating well. Beat in 1 tbsp of the sifted flour, then add the second egg. Mix the almond essence with the milk, add to the mixture then fold in the remainder of the flour.

4. Spread the jam in a thick layer on the pastry case. Sprinkle the grated marzipan on top, and cover with the sponge mixture using a spatula, taking care not to disturb the filling.

5. Make a lattice with the pastry strips over the top and crimp the edges.

6. Bake in a preheated oven at 200°C/400°F/Gas Mark 6 for 20 minutes, then reduce the temperature to 180°C/350°F/Gas Mark 4, and cook for a further 15 minutes until puffed and golden.

TIME: Preparation takes 25 minutes, cooking takes 35 minutes.

Pear Pie Piedmont Style

This is a north Italian dish, and 'Piedmont style' refers to the inclusion of cornmeal in the pastry.

SERVES 6-8

Filling
6 large firm cooking pears
120g/4oz sugar
120ml/4 fl oz red wine
1 whole clove
Pinch cinnamon

Pastry
200g/7oz plain flour
Salt
75g/2½oz yellow cornmeal
150g/5oz caster sugar
120g/4oz butter
3 egg yolks

1. To prepare the filling, peel the pears, then halve and core them. Mix the sugar, wine, clove and cinnamon together in a saucepan. Add the pears, bring to the boil, then simmer for 10-15 minutes or until the pears are almost tender. Remove from the heat and cool.

2. Meanwhile, prepare the pastry. Mix the flour, a pinch of salt, the cornmeal and sugar in a bowl. Rub in the butter until the mixture resembles fine breadcrumbs.

3. Stir in the egg yolks, and if necessary add a little water to make a stiff dough. Knead a couple of times on a floured board, until smooth, then chill for 30 minutes.

4. Roll out two thirds of the dough into a circle large enough to line the bottom and sides of an ungreased 20.5cm/8-inch pie dish.

5. Drain the pears and arrange them on the pastry base. Roll out the remaining pastry to form a lid, and place over the filling. Crimp the edges to seal and prick the top with a fork.

6. Bake in an oven preheated to 220°C/425°F/Gas Mark 7, for 10 minutes, then reduce the heat to 180°C/350°F/Gas Mark 4 and cook for a further 35-40 minutes, or until the pastry is golden brown.

TIME: Preparation takes about 20 minutes plus 30 minutes chilling time. Cooking takes 45-50 minutes.

SERVING IDEA: Serve hot with mascarpone or whipped cream.

Apple Nut Tart

The sweet, spicy flavour of cinnamon blends perfectly with the apples and nuts in this traditional dessert.

SERVES 6

275g/10oz plain flour
150g/5oz caster sugar
150g/5oz butter, cut into pieces
1 egg
460g/1lb dessert apples, peeled, cored and sliced
60g/2oz hazelnuts, coarsely ground
1 tsp ground cinnamon
Juice of 1 lemon
3 tbsps apricot brandy (optional)
75g/4 tbsps apricot jam
60g/2oz chopped hazelnuts

1. Sieve together the flour and 120g/8 tbsps of the sugar into a bowl. Rub in the butter, until the mixture resembles fine breadcrumbs.

2. Make a well in the centre of the flour mixture and drop in the egg. Gradually incorporate the flour into the egg using a knife or, as the mixture becomes firmer, your fingers. Continue kneading the mixture together, until it forms a smooth dough.

3. Wrap the dough in cling film and chill for at least 30 minutes in the refrigerator.

4. Roll out the dough and use it to line a 20.5cm/8-inch greased flan ring.

5. Layer the apple slices and the ground hazelnuts in the pastry case. Sprinkle over the cinnamon, remaining sugar, lemon juice and apricot brandy, if using.

6. Put the apricot jam into a small saucepan and heat through gently until it has melted. Pour the melted jam over the layers of apple and hazelnut.

7. Sprinkle with the chopped hazelnuts and bake in an oven preheated to 220°C/425°F/ Gas Mark 7, for 35-40 minutes, or until the fruit is soft and the tart is golden brown.

TIME: Preparation takes about 20 minutes, and cooking takes about 40 minutes.

SERVING IDEAS: Serve with clotted cream.

TO FREEZE: The tart can be frozen for 6-8 weeks.

ALMOND SAVARIN

Savarins make great centre pieces for cold tables or buffets, and this recipe is ideal for such an occasion as it can be made well in advance and frozen until required.

SERVES 8

225g/8oz plain flour
Pinch salt
2 tsps caster sugar
1 tbsp dried yeast
175ml/6 fl oz lukewarm milk
90g/3oz butter or margarine
4 eggs, beaten
30g/1oz flaked almonds
90g/3oz granulated sugar
140ml/¼ pint water
90ml/6 tbsps Amaretto liqueur
Fresh fruit and whipped cream, to serve

1. Sift the flour and salt into a large bowl and make a well in the centre. Stir the caster sugar and yeast into the warm milk. Pour the yeast mixture into the well and carefully sprinkle a little flour over the top. Leave the bowl in a warm place for about 30 minutes or until the yeast has become very frothy.

2. Carefully mix the flour into the yeast mixture to form a batter, mixing from the centre and gradually incorporating the flour a little at a time from the edges. Soften the butter or margarine and beat into the yeast and flour batter along with the eggs, mixing well until it is shiny and elastic, but still very soft.

3. Thoroughly grease a 20.5cm/8-inch ring or savarin tin and sprinkle the almonds into the tin. Spoon in the batter. Cover with a piece of oiled cling film and leave in a warm place for 30-40 minutes or until the mixture has almost doubled in volume.

4. Bake for about 40 minutes in an oven preheated to 200°C/400°F/Gas Mark 6 until well risen and golden brown. Cool in the tin for a few minutes, then transfer to a wire rack to cool completely.

5. Heat the sugar and water together until the sugar dissolves, then stir in the amaretto. Place the savarin on the rack over a tray and prick all over with a skewer. Spoon the syrup over the savarin, collect any from the tray and spoon over again. Repeat until all the syrup has been absorbed.

6. Serve with fresh fruit and whipped cream.

TIME: Preparation takes about 30 minutes, plus 1 hour proving time. Cooking takes about 40 minutes.

TO FREEZE: After the syrup has been soaked into it, the savarin can be frozen for up to 2 months.

APPLE CAKE

This German apple cake is delicious. Serve warm with whipped cream or vanilla custard.

SERVES 6

Topping
4-6 medium tart apples
Juice of 2 lemons
3 tbsps sugar

Cake
45g/1½oz butter
175g/6oz sugar
2 eggs, separated
Juice and grated zest of ½ lemon
1 tsp baking powder
175g/6oz flour
175ml/6 fl oz milk
1 tbsp rum
1 tsp vegetable oil
3 tbsps icing sugar

1. Peel the apples, cut in half, and core. Cut decorative lengthwise slits in apples, about 1.25cm/½-inch deep (see picture). Sprinkle with lemon juice and sugar. Set aside.

2. To make the cake, cream the butter and sugar together then beat in egg yolks one at a time. Gradually beat in the lemon juice and zest.

3. Sift the baking powder and flour together. Gradually add to the batter. Blend in the milk and rum.

4. In a small bowl beat the egg whites until stiff. Fold into the batter.

5. Generously grease a spring clip cake tin. Pour in the batter and top with the apple halves. Brush the apples with the oil and bake in an oven preheated to 180°C/350°F/Gas Mark 4, for 35-40 minutes.

6. Remove from the tin and sprinkle with icing sugar.

TIME: Preparation takes about 20 minutes and cooking takes 35-40 minutes.

VARIATION: Add a little cinnamon to the flour for extra flavour.

Index